FIZZ

80 joyful cocktails and mocktails
for every occasion

Olly Smith

clarkson potter/publishers
new york

To Ruby & Lily, for when you are old enough!
x Your Proud Dad x

Text copyright © 2020 by Olly Smith

All rights reserved.
Published in the United States by Clarkson Potter/Publishers, an imprint
of Random House, a division of Penguin Random House LLC, New York.
clarksonpotter.com

CLARKSON POTTER is a trademark and POTTER
with colophon is a registered trademark of
Penguin Random House LLC.

Originally published in Great Britain by Ebury Press, an imprint of Ebury
Publishing, a division of Penguin Random House Ltd., London, in 2019.

Library of Congress Cataloging-in-Publication Data
Names: Smith, Olly (Wine writer) author.
Title: Fizz : 80 joyful cocktails and mocktails for every occasion / Olly Smith.
Description: New York : Clarkson Potter, 2020. | Summary: "Here are
    80 seriously simple alcoholic and booze-free cocktails that will help
    you bring joyful moments to the everyday; all you need to do is add
    sparkles. Whether it's champagne, cava, prosecco, cider, beer, tonic,
    soda, ginger ale, or kombucha, these are wonderful bubbly recipes for
    every occasion"—Provided by publisher.
Identifiers: LCCN 2019054135 (print) | LCCN 2019054136 (ebook) |
    ISBN 9780593139448 (hardcover) | ISBN 9780593139455 (ebook)
Subjects: LCSH: Alcoholic beverages. | Non-alcoholic beverages. |
    LCGFT: Cookbooks.
Classification: LCC TX951 .S628 2017 (print) | LCC TX951 (ebook) |
    DDC 641.2/1—dc23
LC record available at https://lccn.loc.gov/2019054135
LC ebook record available at https://lccn.loc.gov/2019054136

ISBN 978-0-593-13944-8
Ebook ISBN 978-0-593-13945-5

Printed in China

10 9 8 7 6 5 4 3 2 1

First American Edition

Introduction

This book is about sharing fun flavors for any occasion in simple cocktail recipes with one thing in common: fizz.

Sparkles are shortcuts to joyful moments. Whether it's champagne, cava, cider, beer, soda, or kombucha, bubbles invariably buzz as we celebrate the occasions, people, and places that are most special to us. With simplicity, these drinks, whether cocktail or mocktail, are designed to take your mood to cruising altitude without the need for takeoff.

THE BASICS

Depending on which fizz you're popping, the drink you're creating will have a unique core characteristic. For instance:

- Classic *champagne* has many merits.
- Mellow fizz such as *prosecco* works with fruity flavors from rhubarb cordial to pomegranate molasses.
- Sour *kombucha* can spritz up zesty tropical flavors such as passion fruit.
- *Cava* is more savory and pairs well with herbal and aromatic ingredients.
- There are *domestic sparkling wines* that you may not know much about.
- The revolution in craft brewing brings its own *beer* frontier breaking across style, depths, and texture.
- The supremacy of *cider* is as yet unsung, with some of the finest and best-value bottle-fermented bargains.
- The salinity of your *soda*, spice of *ginger beer,* or kick of *tonic* sets up the speakers for the other flavors to dance around.
- *Sake* can sparkle and, with high umami and low acidity, lends itself to garden-infused cocktails featuring gentle refreshment, such as cucumber water.

In this book, you'll find out how these all bring the bubbles fizzing into a balance of tantalizing color, flavor, and texture.

To help you pick the right sip for the mood and moment, each mocktail and cocktail is given a three-bar icon rating to indicate how strong the flavors are:

One: Sublime subtlety
Two: Enticing and marvelous
Three: A detonation of deliciousness

There's also an icon to recommend which shape of glass to use for each cocktail, and you'll discover the context in which some of the recipes were introduced onto the world stage. There's also a section with recipes for reductions, syrups, and homemade ingredients, which feature throughout and can be used as the base for the simplest non-alcoholic drinks when topped up with sparkling water.

All the recipes make one drink, except for a few in Parties and Picnics.

TOOLS AND EQUIPMENT

By all means pick and choose from this list, but if you're
serious about getting your fizz in order, these are handy to have.

Grater

Hawthorne strainer

Fine strainer
(or tea strainer)

Muddler (or flat-ended rolling pin)

Chopping board

Boston shaker

1 oz and 2 oz
measures

Fruit knife

Bar spoon
(teaspoon measure
with a long handle)

Lemon
squeezer

Champagne preserver

How bubbles are made has a big impact on the sensation of the drink.

Bottle-fermented drinks such as champagne have smaller bubbles, which gives a more delicate texture. Carbonated drinks such as soda water have larger bubbles, making for a more prickly sensation. And somewhere in the middle, tank-fermented fizz such as prosecco gives the sensation of a caressing cascade.

In this book, I have divided the fabulous fizz flavors into occasions. No need for an invitation; dive in and join me in celebrating the fun of fizz!

Methodology to Mixology

Great ingredients are the cornerstone of superlative cocktails, but how you blend, layer, and mix them is transformative.

These techniques will explain how to turn your cocktail from a mere drink into a delicacy.

SHAKING

Shaking unleashes the fabulous four: mixing, chilling, diluting, and aeration. Shaking ice in the mixture dilutes the mixture as the ice melts. It's a silent ingredient delivering the key to any great cocktail—balance. As the ice cascades around the shaker it chills the liquid. It also unleashes aeration, beating air into the drink. Meanwhile, the liquids are merging and mixing together.

+ TIPPLE TIP

How you shake is key. You're bringing the drink to life, not rocking it to sleep, so you need to apply some elbow grease.

• Always shake out from the shoulder of your strongest arm.
• Extend your weaker arm as you shake.
• Step up the speed, and don't be afraid to really give it some.

A key piece of equipment is the Boston shaker—a glass and a tin. If you have trouble separating them, give the tin part a good squeeze, and the seal should break easily. If still stuck, you'll notice one side where the glass meets the tin is almost flush and the other side has a gap that looks like a grin. Hold the shaker with the gap side toward you and find where the gap just begins on the left-hand side. Using the heel of your left hand, tap the tin where it meets the glass and the gap begins. No need to bash the shaker on the kitchen worktop.

BUILDING

The simple way to make a drink is to pour liquid into a glass, fill with ice, and gently stir. But when topping up with fizz, timing is vital. We've all seen a glass of fizz bubble over if it's poured too quickly, so ice first, fizz next, then stir gently.

+ TIPPLE TIP
When topping up with fizz, always leave room for more ice. If the ice is not touching the bottom of the glass, then more ice is required.

STIRRING

Stirring delivers dilution, chilling, and mixing.

+ TIPPLE TIP
The quality of the ice is vital. If it is fresh out of the freezer, rinse off the frost to prevent your drink from rapidly diluting. Doing so will ensure ice that's crystal clear and solid, helping you to make a perfectly balanced cocktail.

MUDDLING

To extract a juice, oil, or aroma from a fruit or herb, give it a little bashing—or a "muddle." You'll have probably seen limes being muddled for mojitos. Instead of a muddler, you can use a flat-ended rolling pin. Push down onto the fruit or herbs, moving them around gently as you pull up. The juice, oil, and aromas will release—but don't overdo it or you'll bring out bitterness. A little bashing is best.

DRY SHAKE

This is a technique for making cocktails with egg whites. It basically means shaking the drink twice: once to beat air into the mixture and once to dilute and chill the drink.

+ TIPPLE TIP
Always use one single ice cube on your first shake, which helps aerate and keep the shaker sealed. Boston shakers are designed to contract when cold, so if there's nothing cold in there, you risk spilling the contents.

Once the ice cube has stopped rattling, release the tin, fill with ice, and shake again. But only for half as long—too much dilution will spoil all your hard work activating the egg white.

These simple recipes are easy to make in advance not only for the cocktail recipes you'll find in this book but also for customizing your own simple mocktails and experimenting with soft drinks at home. Minimal effort for great satisfaction.

Reductions, Syrups, and Homemade Ingredients

01

Cider Reduction

INGREDIENTS

1 pint dry apple cider   2½ cups sugar   ½ tsp vanilla
                                                        extract

Bring the cider to a boil in a saucepan and add the sugar.
Stir continuously, to prevent the sugar from burning and
the mixture from boiling over, until the sugar has dissolved.
Turn down the heat to low and add the vanilla. Leave to
simmer for around 10 minutes until the liquid starts to
thicken. Leave to cool and decant into a sealable bottle.
Keeps for 2 weeks in the fridge.

Ale and Ginger Reduction

Makes 3 cups

INGREDIENTS

1 pint amber ale   2¼ cups demerara sugar   3½ oz peeled ginger,
                                                           finely grated

Bring the ale to a boil in a large pan and add the sugar,
stirring vigorously to prevent the sugar from burning.
Once the sugar has dissolved, turn down the heat to
low and add the ginger. Simmer for about
10 minutes, then take off the heat and leave
to cool before decanting into a sealable bottle.
Keeps for 1 to 2 weeks in the fridge.

Orange Reduction

Makes 3 cups

INGREDIENTS

1 pint orange juice   2½ cups sugar

Pour the orange juice into a large pan and bring to a boil. Add the sugar and stir continuously to prevent the sugar from burning. Once the sugar has dissolved, take off the heat and leave to cool before decanting into a sealable bottle. Keeps for 1 to 2 weeks in the fridge.

Simple Sugar Syrup

To make more, just stick to equal quantities of sugar and water.

Makes 3 cups

INGREDIENTS

2½ cups sugar   1 pint just-boiled water

Add the sugar to the water in a pan and stir diligently over low heat until all the sugar has dissolved. Leave to cool and then decant into a sealable bottle. Keeps for 3 to 4 weeks in the fridge.

Demerara Sugar Syrup

Makes 3 cups

INGREDIENTS

2¼ cups demerara sugar   1 pint hot water   (equal quantities
to make more)

Add the sugar and the water to a pan and stir over
low heat until all the sugar has dissolved. Leave to cool
and then decant into a sealable bottle. Keeps for
3 to 4 weeks in the fridge.

Pineapple and Cardamom Reduction

Makes 3 cups

INGREDIENTS

1 pint pineapple juice   15 cardamom pods   ½ tsp freshly
2½ cups sugar   ground black pepper

Combine the juice and sugar in a pan. Bring to a
boil, making sure to continuously stir to dissolve the
sugar. Turn down the heat to a simmer and add the
spices. Leave to simmer for 10 minutes, then take
off the heat. Leave to cool. Strain out the spices
and then decant into a sealable bottle.
Keeps for 1 to 2 weeks in the fridge.

Cranberry Reduction

INGREDIENTS

1 pint cranberry juice   2½ cups sugar

Pour the cranberry juice into a large pan and bring to a boil. Add the sugar and stir continuously to prevent it from burning. Once the sugar has dissolved, take off the heat and leave to cool before decanting into a sealable bottle. Keeps for 1 to 2 weeks in the fridge.

Cranberry and Vanilla Reduction: Simply add ½ teaspoon vanilla extract to the mix.

Spiced Mango Reduction

Makes 3 cups

INGREDIENTS

10 oz mango juice   2½ cups sugar   2 large cinnamon
7 oz apple juice   15 cardamom pods   sticks

Combine the juices and sugar in a large pan and bring to a boil, making sure to continuously stir to dissolve the sugar. Turn down the heat to a simmer and add the spices. Leave to simmer for 10 minutes, then take off the heat. Leave to cool. Strain out the spices and then decant into a sealable bottle. Keeps for 1 to 2 weeks in the fridge.

Strawberry and Black Pepper Fizz

This makes an amazing cordial to add to any fizz or sparkling water for a quick and scrumptious booze-free bubbly.

<u>Makes 1½ quarts</u>

INGREDIENTS

3⅓ cups frozen strawberries, defrosted

1 tbsp whole black peppercorns

1 lemon, thinly sliced

4½ cups sugar

1 pint water

3 tbsp citric acid

In a large pan, combine the strawberries, peppercorns, lemon, and sugar. Place over medium heat, making sure you keep stirring to prevent the sugar from burning. Add the water and stir until the sugar has completely dissolved.

Take off the heat and add the citric acid, stirring until dissolved. Leave to cool and then transfer to the fridge to chill for 2 to 3 days.

Strain all the fruit and decant into a sealable bottle. Keeps for 1 to 2 weeks in the fridge.

+ TIPPLE TIP For the recipes in this book that contain this homemade strawberry and black pepper concentrate, the proportions that work best are one part cordial to five parts sparkling water. But you can, of course, adjust these ratios to your taste.

Oleo Saccharum

A homemade liquid sherbet, similar to a fresh citrus cordial.
Gorgeous to use across the board in sparkling cocktails, or to top
up with sparkling water for an invigorating non-alcoholic fizz.
Try a few drops in salad dressings too—it tastes superb!

<u>Makes about 1 quart</u>

INGREDIENTS

10 lemons	2 grapefruits	3 cups sugar
	2 oranges	

Peel the lemons, grapefruits, and oranges (I use a veggie
peeler) and place the peels into a large metal bowl. Reserve
the fruit and keep in the fridge for later. Add the sugar and,
with a muddler or flat-ended rolling pin, bash the sugar
into the peels. Do this for about 15 minutes, cover with
plastic wrap, and leave for 24 hours in a cool, dry place.

Every so often, feel free to go back and bash the peels a bit
more to help them release their oils into the sugar. Once
you have a very thick syrup, juice the lemons, oranges, and
grapefruits, and add to the mix. Stir and then strain. Decant
into a sealable bottle. Keeps for 1 to 2 weeks in the fridge.

Everyone needs the basics in their locker,
and these fizz sensations
deliver the simplest ways to create
a range of classics at home.

Easy
Classics

02

INGREDIENTS

1 brown sugar cube
3 dashes of
Angostura bitters
1 oz sweet vermouth
champagne

GLASS

Champagne flute

GARNISH

Orange peel or zest

Alfonso

This enticing sparkling wonder was first created
in Paris in the 1930s for the deposed Spanish king
Alfonso XIII, who was exiled in France. Banish your
troubles with this barrage of bubbles, a variation
on the classic champagne cocktail.

Soak the brown sugar cube in Angostura bitters and
drop into the glass. Add the vermouth and top with
champagne, pouring carefully to avoid frothing over.
Garnish with a twist of orange peel or some zest.

INGREDIENTS	**GLASS**	**GARNISH**
1 oz Campari	Rocks or	Chunky slice
1 oz sweet vermouth	small tumbler	of orange
ice cubes		
prosecco		

Negroni Sbagliato

A happy mistake from Milan when legendary
bartender Mirko Stocchetto accidentally picked up
a bottle of sparkling wine when reaching for his gin.

Pour the Campari and sweet vermouth into the glass
and fill with ice. Top with prosecco and gently stir to
mix. Garnish with a chunky orange slice.

1 lime wedge or
1 tsp freshly squeezed
lime juice

2 oz London dry gin

ice cubes

5 oz tonic water,
the best you can find

Collins or highball

Wedge of lime

Gin and Tonic

The most famous highball in the world. With so
many uniquely crafted gins and premium tonic
waters now sloshing across every bar in the world,
if I were to share with you the perfect serve for all
of them, there wouldn't be any space for any other
drinks. So I'm going to reveal my greatest gin and
tonic while keeping things splendidly simple.

Squeeze the lime juice into the glass and discard
the wedge, if using. Pour in the gin and fill the glass
to the top with ice cubes. Top with premium-quality
tonic water and garnish with a fresh wedge of lime.

INGREDIENTS
4 tsp peach purée
non-alcoholic
sparkling wine

GLASS
Champagne flute

GARNISH
None

Virgin Bellini

(Booze Free)

Something that allows you to enjoy the flavor
and feel of drinking a classic Bellini but without the
booze! Sip wild, sip free, and get involved with as
many of these as you can muster.

Pour the peach purée into the glass, roll around in
the glass, and top with the non-alcoholic sparkling wine.

INGREDIENTS
1 oz orange juice
2 tsp triple sec
sparkling apple cider

GLASS
Champagne flute

GARNISH
Slice of apple

Cider Mimosa

An upbeat modification on the classic mimosa,
swapping out champagne for a sparkling cider
to give a bolder and altogether fruitier body.

Pour the orange juice and triple sec into the glass and
top with the apple cider. Garnish with a slice of apple.

INGREDIENTS

1 oz vanilla vodka

4 tsp passion
fruit liqueur

1 oz passion
fruit purée

2 tsp vanilla sugar

ice cubes

GLASS

Martini

GARNISH

½ passion fruit and
a shot of prosecco

Pornstar Martini

Due to its enduring popularity, the pornstar martini belongs in the pantheon of modern-day classics. Created by Douglas Ankrah in 2002, this is a slightly unusual sparkling cocktail with the fizz served on the side. Party time!

Pour the vodka, passion fruit liqueur, passion fruit purée, and vanilla sugar into a Boston shaker. Fill with ice cubes and shake until the tin is cold. Fine strain into the glass. Garnish the drink with half a passion fruit and pour a shot of prosecco to serve on the side.

INGREDIENTS

1 lime wedge

ice cubes

6 juniper berries

dash of Peychaud's
bitters or similar

1 lemon wedge

tonic water

GLASS

Highball or collins

GARNISH

Cucumber slice sprinkled
with black sesame seeds

Hoxton Tonic

(Nearly Booze Free)

This mighty semi-mocktail was crafted for me
in the beautiful bar at The Hoxton in Paris by their
splendid team on a visit with my daughter Ruby.
I'm smiling at the very thought of it.

Tuck the lime wedge at the bottom of the glass and add
a couple of ice cubes. Crush the juniper berries and
add a dash of Peychaud's bitters. Add more ice
cubes and a drop of lemon juice from the wedge,
and top up with decent tonic water. (To make it
totally booze free, leave out the bitters.)
Add the cucumber and sesame seed garnish.

INGREDIENTS	**GLASS**	**GARNISH**
1 brown sugar cube	Champagne flute	Twist of orange peel
3 dashes of Angostura bitters		
1 oz VS cognac		
champagne		

Classic Champagne Cocktail

Legend has it that this iconic cocktail stretches back to the mid-1800s. The story goes that it began with an 1806 definition of a cocktail found in *The Balance, and Columbian Repository,* where we learn that a "cocktail is a stimulating liquor composed of spirit of any kind, sugar, water, and bitters, vulgarly called a bittered sling." In this case the water is turned into wine—champagne, no less—but this recipe also works a charm with any other zesty fizz.

Soak the brown sugar cube in Angostura bitters and drop into the glass. Add the cognac and top with champagne. Take good care and pour gently as the bubbles love to get lively when mixing with the sugar! Add the twist of orange peel.

INGREDIENTS	**GLASS**	**GARNISH**
2½ oz Guinness	Champagne flute	None
splash of champagne, crémant, or cava		

Black Velvet

First created by the bartender of Brooks's Club, London, in 1861 to mourn the death of Prince Albert, Queen Victoria's Prince Consort. The coffee notes from the stout blend beautifully with the cookie depth of champagne, but it works just as well with crémant or a Spanish cava. It may have been designed for a moment of mourning, but its tremendous taste is well worth celebrating.

Simply pour the Guinness into the glass and top with the champagne.

INGREDIENTS

1 lemon wedge or 1 tsp freshly squeezed lemon juice

2 oz white port

ice cubes

5 oz Fever-Tree Premium Indian tonic water or other premium-quality tonic water of choice

GLASS

Collins or highball

GARNISH

Wedge of orange

White Port and Tonic

On my many wine trips to Portugal, I've always adored this twist on our G&T. There's nothing finer than savoring the views over the Douro Valley vineyards with a glass of this cool golden glory in one hand and some salted almonds in the other.

Squeeze the lemon juice into the glass and discard the wedge, if using. Pour in the port and fill the glass to the top with ice cubes. Top with the tonic water, and garnish with a fresh wedge of orange.

These zesty apéritifs are designed to treat your tastebuds like royalty! With all the excitement and anticipation of a red carpet event, they set the scene for epic adventures to come. Take a bow and advance into apéro!

Apéro!

03

INGREDIENTS

1 oz Italicus bergamot
liqueur
or similar

2 tsp lemon juice

3 to 4 sprigs of
lemon thyme

ice cubes

prosecco

GLASS

Highball or collins

GARNISH

Lemon peel, sprig
of lemon thyme

A Little Thyme in Italy

Italicus, a fabulous floral liqueur, couldn't taste
more Italian. With authentic bergamot and native
botanicals, its alluring citrus scent and lingering
nuances of rose and lavender are the perfect
canvas for sketching out this beautiful apéritif.

Combine the bergamot liqueur, lemon juice, and lemon
thyme together in a Boston shaker filled with ice cubes.
Shake until the tin is cold. Fine strain into the glass
filled with more ice cubes. Top with prosecco, then
garnish with a lemon peel and sprig of lemon thyme.

1 tsp elderflower cordial
1 tsp lime cordial
drop of orange blossom
water
soda water, chilled

Champagne flute

None

Sham-pagne

(Booze Free)

This looks like a glass of classy champagne and tastes divine.
Perfect for going booze free at a party.

Pour the elderflower and lime cordials into your champagne
flute, add a drop of orange blossom water, and
top up with ice-cold soda water. Stir gently. Adjust
the flavor, adding more cordials to your taste.

INGREDIENTS

1 oz manzanilla sherry
2 tsp lemon juice
1 tbsp peach schnapps
ice cubes
cava

GLASS

Coupette or champagne
saucer

GARNISH

Lemon peel

Spanish Peaches

Anticipating the flurry of a fiesta, this drink shows off the splendor of Spain. Try using Teichenné, a peach schnapps from Mediterranean Barcelona, sherry from southern Jerez, and cava, Spain's signature bubbly. Olé!

Combine the sherry, lemon juice, and peach schnapps in a Boston shaker. Fill with ice cubes and shake until the tin is cold. Strain the shaken mixture into the glass and top with cava. Add the lemon peel garnish.

INGREDIENTS	GLASS	GARNISH
1 oz LoneWolf gin or similar	Wine	Wedge of grapefruit
2 oz freshly squeezed grapefruit juice		
1 tsp crème de violette		
ice cubes		
1 tsp Luxardo Maraschino		
champagne		

Hemingway's Aviation

Inspired by two classic cocktails: the Hemingway Daiquiri and the Aviation. By using the floral flourishes from the Aviation's fusion of gin, violet, and maraschino with the bitter twist of Hemingway's maraschino and grapefruit, this invigorating apéritif is elegantly elongated with champagne.

Combine the gin, grapefruit juice, violet liqueur, and maraschino in a Boston shaker. Fill with ice cubes and shake until cold. Strain the shaken mixture into the glass filled with some more cubed ice. Top with champagne and garnish with a wedge of grapefruit.

+ TIPPLE TIP Any London dry gin can be used in this, but LoneWolf from Scotland works a treat with its aromatic citrus botanicals of lemongrass, lime leaf, and pink grapefruit.

INGREDIENTS

GLASS

GARNISH

4 tsp Aperol or similar
1 tsp lemon juice
ice cubes
light pale ale

Rocks

Slice of orange

Pale Aperale

The Aperol spritz has taken the world by storm, and while Italy's very own Aperol has taken on near ritual status, this little number is lengthened with a light pale ale, giving a subtle tropical twist and hoppy boost.

Pour the Aperol and lemon juice into the glass filled with ice cubes. Top with a light pale ale and gently stir. Garnish with a slice of orange.

INGREDIENTS

1 oz Martins de
Sá rosé port or similar of
your choice

1 oz freshly pressed
pineapple juice

2 tsp lime juice

dash of orange bitters

ice cubes

prosecco

GLASS

Coupette or champagne
saucer

GARNISH

Orange peel, thin wedge
of pineapple

Port and Pineapple

Port from Portugal is a world of craft, tradition, and
innovation, and I passionately believe it should be
showcased far more in the cocktail world. In fact,
we should all be drinking more port, period, but this
particular rosé port is a romp of a drink, all cherry
and sweet citrus with electrifying intensity. Mixed
with tropical fruits and drawn out with prosecco, this
fruity concoction will send your tastebuds soaring.

Combine the port and the pineapple and lime juices along
with the orange bitters in a Boston shaker. Fill with ice cubes
and shake until the tin is cold. Strain the shaken mixture
into the glass, top with prosecco, and garnish with the
orange peel and pineapple wedge.

INGREDIENTS

1 oz freshly squeezed
grapefruit juice

4 tsp Oleo Saccharum
(see page 15)

ice cubes

soda water

GLASS

White wine

GARNISH

Large grapefruit peel

Sherbet Fizz

(Booze Free)

The aromatic sweetness of the homemade
Oleo Saccharum pairs fantastically here with the
bitterness of grapefruit. Lifted by the bubbles and salty
subtlety of soda water, it's a buzzing beauty.

Pour the grapefruit juice and Oleo Saccharum into
the glass filled with ice cubes, top with soda water,
and stir gently. Garnish with a grapefruit peel.

INGREDIENTS

2 oz dry vermouth

1 tsp lemon juice

dash of orange blossom
water

ice cubes

Franklin & Sons
elderflower with
cucumber tonic water

Frenchie and Tonic

Floral French vermouth, in particular Noilly Prat, pairs beautifully with elderflower and cucumber tonic water. The cucumber adds an additional freshness to the drink, which is lifted with a touch of lemon and perfumed with orange blossom water.

Combine the dry vermouth, lemon juice, and orange blossom water in the wine glass filled with ice cubes. Top with the elderflower and cucumber tonic water and garnish with a slice of cucumber.

INGREDIENTS

4 tsp Campari
or similar

4 tsp freshly squeezed
orange juice

ice cubes

splash of dry
apple cider

GLASS

Collins or highball

GARNISH

Wedge of orange

Apple Campers

Campari is one of my favorites. With its intense, invigorating flavor and wonderfully alluring deep-fuchsia color, the bitter orange, grapefruit, and fragrant herbs and spices fit splendidly together like the perfect liquid jigsaw. And pairing these flavors with a dry apple cider creates another dimension to a classic apéritif.

Pour the Campari and orange juice into the glass filled with ice cubes. Top with a dry apple cider and gently stir. Garnish with a wedge of orange.

INGREDIENTS

1½ oz sake

2 tsp pomegranate cordial

ice cubes

good-quality ginger ale

GLASS

Collins or highball

GARNISH

Large twirl of lemon peel and orange peel, entwined

Orange Sake

Sake has a beautiful fruity as well as umami flavor. It's quite savory—spot on to unleash between a spark of gingery warmth and earthy, fruity pomegranate.

Stir the sake and pomegranate cordial over ice to mix; set aside. Fill another glass with ice cubes and place the garnish around the ice. Pour in the sake-pomegranate mix and top up with good-quality ginger ale.

With the robust and satisfying richness
of digéstifs, these potions are prepared
to prime your conversation.

Fizz for
Feasts

04

1 oz Manchester
raspberry gin or similar
gin of choice

4 tsp half-and-half

1 tsp lemon juice

ice cubes

Brachetto d'Acqui (sweet
sparkling Italian pink
fizz) or similar

Wine

Slice of strawberry,
a raspberry,
lemon peel

Eton Fizz

Inspired by the fruity fun of Eton Mess, the fruity botanicals
of Manchester gin offer a fine foundation for building an
enticingly sweet summery stunner with Brachetto d'Acqui
as wine's answer to sherbet.

Combine the gin, half-and-half, and lemon juice in a Boston
shaker. Fill with ice cubes and shake until the tin is cold.
Fine strain into the glass filled with more ice cubes. Top with
the Brachetto d'Acqui and gently stir. Garnish with a sliced
strawberry, a raspberry, and a sliver of lemon peel.

INGREDIENTS
4 tsp Ale and
Ginger Reduction
(see page 10)
4 tsp apple juice
2 tsp lemon juice
ice cubes
prosecco

GLASS
Sling

GARNISH
Apple fan

Remember the 5th of November

The Ale and Ginger Reduction imbues a sweet burnished depth, which tastes just like caramel apples.

Combine the Ale and Ginger Reduction with the apple and lemon juices in a Boston shaker. Fill with ice cubes and shake until the tin is cold. Strain into the glass filled with more cubed ice and top with prosecco. Give it a gentle stir to mix and then garnish with an apple fan.

INGREDIENTS

ice cubes

good-quality
ginger ale (such
as Fever-Tree)

a decent India Pale Ale

dash of Simple Sugar
Syrup (see page 11)

GLASS

Tulip-shaped beer

GARNISH

Wedges of lemon,
wedges of lime,
fresh mint leaves

Craft Shandy

Traditionally, shandy is half beer and half lemonade,
but here I've created a summery explosion of wild
mint with great craft beer that's also easy on
the alcohol—perfect for a cooling summer session.

Build wedges of fresh lemon and lime up through the
beer glass. Fill with ice cubes, packing the fresh
mint around it. Pour in 2 parts ginger ale to 1 part
beer and a dash of Simple Sugar Syrup to taste.

INGREDIENTS
1 whole egg
4 tsp half-and-half
4 tsp almond syrup
2 oz cognac
ice cubes
2 oz soda water

GLASS
Tumbler or rocks

GARNISH
Toasted sliced almonds

Almonds and Cream

Light and rich at the same time, the peachy flavor
of cognac balances with the sweet almond syrup,
creating a fruit-and-nut base that's enhanced with
the texture of half-and-half and lightened with soda.

In this order, combine the egg, half-and-half, almond syrup,
and cognac in a Boston shaker. Add one ice cube and shake
until the ice cube has completely dissolved. Keep the liquid
in the glass of your Boston shaker and fill the tin section
with ice cubes. Shake the mixture again until the tin is cold.

Pour the soda into the tumbler and fine strain the
shaken mixture into the glass. This should create a fair
amount of foam, but it should still be light when you taste it.
Sprinkle toasted sliced almonds on top.

INGREDIENTS
4 tsp Ale and
Ginger Reduction
(see page 10)
4 tsp caramel syrup
1 tsp lemon juice
1 whole egg
4 tsp half-and-half
ice cubes
2 oz soda water

GLASS
Half-pint

GARNISH
None

Nothing but a Butter Beer

(Booze Free)

Potter! Taking inspiration from Harry Potter while riffing on the classic flip cocktail (a base shaken with egg and sweetened by sugar), this is both indulgent and light. And although it contains the Ale and Ginger Reduction, as the syrup boils the alcohol evaporates, leaving it booze free. Magic!

Combine the Ale and Ginger Reduction, caramel syrup, lemon juice, egg, and half-and-half in a Boston shaker. Fill with ice cubes and shake until the tin is cold. In a half-pint glass, pour in the soda water and fine strain the shaken mixture over the soda. This should give a froth resembling a tasty half-pint of beer—but in this case, minus the booze.

INGREDIENTS
1 oz Scotch
2 tsp lemon juice
dash of orange bitters
sparkling gooseberry
wine (such as
Cairn o'Mohr)

GLASS
Champagne flute

GARNISH
Orange peel or slice of
dehydrated orange

Highland Goose

A twist on the French 75, but instead of dry, clean, zesty freshness, this cocktail delivers more richness and body from the Scotch as well as fruity zip from the gooseberry wine.

Combine the Scotch, lemon juice, bitters, and sparkling wine in the champagne flute. Give it a gentle stir, being careful not to aggravate the sparkling wine. Garnish with orange peel.

INGREDIENTS

2 oz aged rum

2 tsp Demerara Sugar
Syrup (see page 12)

2 dashes of spiced apple
bitters

ice cubes

1 oz dry apple cider

GLASS

Rocks glass or tumbler

GARNISH

Slice of apple

One for You, Treacle

Adapted from the classic rum cocktail, the Treacle,
created by Dick Bradsell, this recipe switches the
traditional apple juice for a combination of
spiced apple bitters and a dry cider, doubling
the dimension of appley awesomeness.

Add the rum, Demerara Sugar Syrup, and bitters
to the glass. Half-fill with ice cubes and stir until
mixed. Top up with more ice and add the cider. Stir
a little more and garnish with a slice of apple.

INGREDIENTS

1 oz half-and-half

1 tsp honey

1 tbsp toasted oats

ice cubes

Strawberry and
Black Pepper Fizz
(see page 14)

GLASS

Champagne flute

GARNISH

Slice of strawberry,
toasted oats

Strawberries and Cream

(Booze Free)

This non-alcoholic mixture is a contemplative,
fruity, and delicious digéstif thanks to the rich
cream and toasted oats.

Combine the half-and-half, honey, and oats in a Boston
shaker. Fill with ice cubes and shake until the tin is cold.
Fine strain into the champagne flute and top with the
Strawberry and Black Pepper Fizz. Garnish with a slice
of strawberry and toasted oats. Yummy!

INGREDIENTS

2 oz spiced rum

1 oz freshly pressed
pineapple juice

2 tsp coconut purée
(such as Coco Reàl
cream of coconut)

2 tsp Spiced
Mango Reduction
(see page 13)

2 tsp lime juice

ice cubes

cava

GLASS

Sling

GARNISH

Pineapple leaf,
slice of lime

Coco Cabana Spritz

This tropical tantalizer unites a sling (spirit
mixed with sugar and water) and the iconic piña
colada with the extra might of mango.

Combine the spiced rum, pineapple juice, coconut purée,
Spiced Mango Reduction, and lime juice in a Boston shaker.
Fill with ice cubes and shake until the tin is cold. Fine strain
the mixture into a glass filled with more cubed ice and
top with cava. Give it a gentle stir to mix in the cava, and
garnish with a pineapple leaf and slice of lime.

INGREDIENTS	GLASS	GARNISH
1 oz egg white 1 oz lemon juice 1 tbsp Simple Sugar Syrup (see page 11) 2 oz bourbon ice cubes good-quality ginger beer (such as Franklin & Sons)	Rocks glass or tumbler	Crumbled graham crackers, orange peel

Englishman in Kentucky

This cocktail tastes like liquid gingerbread! In particular, Franklin and Sons ginger beer—with its malted barley—gives the taste of a cookie base with a warming gingery boost, but you can always use any good-quality ginger beer instead. With its velvety and smooth texture you could serve this tipple as a dessert or anytime you feel like some delicious indulgence.

In this order, combine the egg white, lemon juice, Simple Sugar Syrup, and bourbon in a Boston shaker. Add one ice cube and shake until the ice cube has completely dissolved. Keep the liquid in the glass of your Boston shaker and fill the tin section with ice cubes. Pour in the liquid, and shake again until the tin turns cold. Pour the ginger beer into the glass and fine strain the shaken mixture over the top. This creates a scrumptious foam that's lovely and light.

Smash up some graham crackers and sprinkle on top. For aroma, cut a small disc of orange peel from the side of a fresh orange and spray it over the drink by squeezing—peel side facing the drink.

With simplicity and batch-making at their core, these social pitcher drinks are designed to transform moments into occasions.

Parties
and Picnics

05

INGREDIENTS

1 oz London dry gin

1 oz Cocchi Rosa
or similar

2 tsp lemon juice

2 oz freshly pressed
pomegranate juice

ice cubes

dry apple cider

GLASS

Large wine

GARNISH

Slices of apple,
pomegranate seeds
(optional)

Rosy Apples

Think of this splendid drink as a cider spritz. The
grapefruit and rose scent of Cocchi Rosa matched
with the dry pomegranate and tangy cider concocts
a sharing cocktail with a delightful spring in its step.

Pour the gin, Cocchi Rosa, and lemon and pomegranate juices
into the glass filled with ice cubes. Top with apple cider and
garnish with an apple fan and pomegranate seeds, if using.

TO MAKE A LARGE BATCH

Add 8 oz gin, 8 oz Cocchi Rosa, 3 oz lemon juice, and 1 pint
freshly pressed pomegranate juice to a 2-quart pitcher and
top with a dry apple cider. Give it a gentle stir to mix the
ingredients and pour into wineglasses filled with ice cubes.

INGREDIENTS

8 to 10 mint leaves

2 oz London dry gin

1 tbsp lemon juice

4 tsp elderflower cordial

ice cubes

sparkling wine

GLASS

Large wine

GARNISH

Sprig of mint, slice
of lemon

English Summer Highball

A light and refreshing highball that's great for sunny
days to show off the zing of sparkling wine.
(Pictured: a large batch.)

Add the mint leaves to the glass and pour in the gin, lemon
juice, and elderflower cordial. Fill the glass with ice cubes and
top with sparkling wine. Give the drink a gentle stir to mix
and garnish with a sprig of mint and a slice of lemon.

TO MAKE A LARGE BATCH

Take a 2-quart pitcher and combine 1 pint London dry gin,
5 oz lemon juice, 7 oz elderflower cordial, a handful of fresh
mint leaves, and slices of lemon and top with the sparkling
wine. Give it a gentle stir to mix the ingredients before
pouring into glasses filled with ice. Garnish each
glass with a sprig of mint and a slice of lemon.

INGREDIENTS

2 oz freshly pressed
pomegranate juice

1 oz Oleo Saccharum
(see page 15)

2 tsp lemon juice

ice cubes

good-quality
ginger ale

GLASS

Highball or collins

GARNISH

Slice of lemon,
pomegranate seeds

Punchless Punch

(Booze Free)

A gloriously fresh non-alcoholic punch. Working
to a similar principle as spiced rum but majoring
on warming flavors instead of boozy depth.

Add the pomegranate juice, Oleo Saccharum, and
lemon juice to the glass. Fill with ice and top with
ginger ale. Give the drink a little stir and garnish
with a slice of lemon and pomegranate seeds.

TO MAKE A LARGE BATCH

Fill a 2-quart pitcher with 1 pint freshly pressed
pomegranate juice, 8 oz Oleo Saccharum, and 3 oz
lemon juice and then top with ginger ale. Give it
a stir to mix the ingredients, and serve in glasses
filled with ice cubes. Garnish as above.

4 tsp VS cognac

Gin copa

Slices of orange, lemon,
and apple

4 tsp sweet
vermouth (such as
Dubonnet Rouge)

2 tsp Cider Reduction
(see page 10)

2 tsp lemon juice

ice cubes

good-quality
ginger ale

Orchard Picnic Cup

Superb for the last few days of summer.

Combine the cognac, sweet vermouth, Cider Reduction,
and lemon juice in the glass. Give it a little mix with a spoon
and start alternately building your fruit and ice until the
glass is full. Then just top up with ginger ale and give it a
stir. Finish off with more ice and garnish with a little more
of the fruit. The more fruit in this drink the better!

TO MAKE A LARGE BATCH

Fill a 2-quart pitcher with 7 oz cognac, 7 oz sweet vermouth,
3 oz Cider Reduction, and 2 oz lemon juice and give it a stir.
Add fruit and ice alternately and then top with ginger ale and
stir to mix the ingredients. Finish off with more ice
and garnish with a little more of the fruit.

INGREDIENTS
ice cubes
mint leaves
2 oz fino sherry (Tío
Pepe works like a charm)
4 oz lemon-lime soda
(such as 7UP or Sprite)

GLASS
Highball or collins

GARNISH
Slice of
lemon (optional)

Rebujito

This is the drink that keeps the feria dancing in Spain's Jerez
in spring—utterly scrumptious and showcases
sherry at the heart of this beautiful batch cocktail.

Fill your glass with ice cubes and fresh mint, then pour
in fino sherry and top up with 7UP or Sprite. Add more
cubed ice, and a lemon slice to garnish is optional. Dance!

TO MAKE A LARGE BATCH

Follow the above proportions (one part fino sherry
to two parts fizz) and combine all the ingredients in
a 2-quart pitcher. You'll need to make another pitcher
very quickly—this stuff vanishes like music in the night.

INGREDIENTS

2 oz spiced rum

4 tsp lime juice

1 oz mango juice

1 oz green tea, chilled

4 tsp Oleo Saccharum
(see page 15)

ice cubes

cava (non-vintage)

GLASS

Sling

GARNISH

Wedge of lime,
sprig of mint

Sparkling Rum Punch

Punch originally comes from *panch*, the Hindi word for "five," reflecting the drink's five key tenets: strong, weak, sweet, sour, and spiced. This recipe builds around the combination of mango, green tea, and cava, which work in perfect harmony, thanks to their comparable levels of intensity. (Pictured: a large batch.)

In the glass, build the rum, lime and mango juices, cold green tea, and Oleo Saccharum. Fill the glass with ice and top with cava. Give it a gentle stir to mix and then garnish with a wedge of lime and a mint sprig.

TO MAKE A LARGE BATCH

Take a 2-quart pitcher and combine 1 pint spiced rum, 7 oz freshly squeezed lime juice, 8 oz mango juice, 8 oz cold green tea, and 7 oz Oleo Saccharum and top with cava. Give the mixture a gentle stir and pour into glasses filled with ice.

INGREDIENTS

1 oz vodka

1 tbsp lemon juice

1 oz Lillet Blanc
or similar

2 tsp Cranberry
Reduction (see
page 13)

ice cubes

prosecco

GLASS

Gin copa

GARNISH

Lemon peel

Water into Wine

Vodka's origin comes from the Russian for "little water,"
and here it's blended with aromatized and sparkling
wine. Simple and jolly scrumptious!

In the glass, combine the vodka, lemon juice, Lillet Blanc, and
Cranberry Reduction. Take a large peel of lemon and stick
it to the inside of the glass using the back of the spoon.
Fill the glass with ice cubes and top with prosecco. Give
a gentle stir, but be careful not to disturb the garnish.

TO MAKE A LARGE BATCH

Fill a 2-quart pitcher with 8 oz vodka, 5 oz lemon juice,
8 oz Lillet Blanc, and 3 oz Cranberry Reduction and
top up with prosecco. Give it a gentle stir to mix the
ingredients and pour into glasses filled with cubed ice.

INGREDIENTS

ice cubes

1 oz Mandarine
Napoléon or similar

2 tsp lemon juice

2 oz freshly squeezed
orange juice

Tenuta di Aljano
Settefilari Lambrusco
Reggiano DOP
(or your choice
of sparkling
red Lambrusco)

GLASS

Large wine

GARNISH

Slices of orange, lemon,
and apple

Napoléon's Sangria

This cocktail is as joyful and bright as an orange
the size of the sun. With huge surging tides of
orange flavor, thanks to a combination of Mandarine
Napoléon and freshly squeezed orange, it's a nod
to sangria with sparkling red wine.

Pop a few slices of orange, lemon, and apple into the
glass. Add a little ice and repeat until the glass is full.
Pour in the Mandarine Napoléon, lemon and orange
juices, and Lambrusco. Give it a gentle stir. Garnish
with a slice of orange, slice of lemon, and slice of apple.

TO MAKE A LARGE BATCH

In a 2-quart pitcher, combine 8 oz Mandarine Napoléon,
3 oz lemon juice, and 1 pint orange juice, then top with
fizzy red Lambrusco. Give it a gentle stir to mix the
ingredients and then pour into glasses filled with
fruit slices and ice cubes. Sunny splendor!

INGREDIENTS

3¾ quarts water

2 heaped tsp green tea leaves or 2 green tea bags

2 tsp jasmine tea leaves or 2 jasmine tea bags

1 cup sugar

8 oz kombucha (previously made or store-bought)

1 scoby

gingerroot, peeled

GLASS

Flip-top bottles

MAKES

About 3¾ quarts

Ginger Kombucha

(Booze Free)

My friend Jamie, who runs Bun and Bean in Lewes, East Sussex, gave me a scoby to start making kombucha. Scobys (symbiotic cultures of bacteria and yeast) can be sourced from those who make kombucha or bought online. It is claimed that kombucha makes you happy, is good for your gut, and is packed with health-giving loveliness. All I can say is that this natural fizz tastes superb!

Bring the water to a boil in a large pan. Add the green and jasmine teas and sugar. Stir to mix until the sugar is completely dissolved. Remove from the heat and allow to cool.

Place your cooled tea mixture in a big jar. Add the kombucha and scoby. Cover with a clean tea towel and secure with a rubber band. Leave for 1 week or so out of direct sunlight. Taste toward the end of the week, when a film should have developed over the surface—this is a new scoby growing. If it's too sharp, you've left it too long; too sweet, and it needs more time. The bubbles are perfect when at their most effervescent.

Pour the kombucha into sturdy flip-top
bottles with a piece of gingerroot (around half
a finger long) in each bottle and keep in the fridge
until you're ready to pop your feel-good fizz!

INGREDIENTS

ice cubes

1 oz London dry gin

1 oz sweet vermouth (such as Dubonnet Rouge)

1 tsp lemon juice

2½ oz Franklin & Sons wild strawberry and Scottish raspberry with cracked black pepper soft drink or homemade Strawberry and Black Pepper Fizz (see page 14)

2 oz Brachetto d'Acqui or similar

GLASS

Gin copa

GARNISH

Slices of lemon, strawberry slices, a whole raspberry, freshly ground black pepper

Wine-Up Fruit Cup

Pimms is a popular well-known version of the fruit cup. Making your own version is easier than you think. Starting with a base of gin and sweet vermouth, flavors are boosted with summery strawberries and raspberries, plus Brachetto d'Acqui for an extra layer of fruit.

In the glass, pop in a few slices of lemon and slice up some strawberries. Add a little ice and repeat until the glass is full. Pour in the gin, vermouth, lemon juice, and Strawberry and Black Pepper Fizz and give the drink a gentle stir. Top up with the Brachetto d'Acqui. Garnish with a slice of lemon, a whole strawberry sliced and fanned, raspberries, and some freshly ground black pepper for aroma.

TO MAKE A LARGE BATCH

In a 2-quart pitcher, combine 8 oz gin, 8 oz sweet vermouth, 2 oz lemon juice, 3 cups Strawberry and Black Pepper Fizz, and 1 pint Brachetto d'Acqui. Give it a gentle stir to mix the ingredients. Pour the mixture into glasses filled with lemon slices, whole strawberries and raspberries, and cubed ice and top each with black pepper.

These exotic fruit-fueled beauties
amp up the mood and tempo,
bringing the flavors of faraway
places right to your front door.

Holidays
at Home

06

INGREDIENTS

crushed ice

2 oz passion
fruit juice

2 oz pineapple juice

2 oz mango juice

1 lime

1 orange

long thin wedge of fresh
pineapple, skin removed

1 oz Frobishers
peach and lychee
cordial or similar

1 oz bottlegreen ginger
and lemongrass cordial
or similar

3 oz sparkling
elderflower, chilled

GLASS

Hurricane

GARNISH

Thin slice
of pineapple

Fruit Bonanza

(Booze Free)

This is an outrageous fruit festival as tropical and punchy
as it is sweet and fragrant—the perfect recipe to transport
your taste buds to instant holidays.

Put heaps of crushed ice into the glass. Add the juices
one by one to the ice, building the cocktail steadily. Make a
"cheek" of lime by cutting off one side of the fruit and add
it to the glass. Slice a cheek of orange and add to
the glass. Add the wedge of pineapple.

Pour the cordials into the glass and stir to mix all together.
Top up with sparkling elderflower and give the drink
another gentle stir. Garnish with an extra-thin slice
of pineapple and add to the side of the glass.

INGREDIENTS

1 oz tequila blanco

1 tbsp lime juice

4 tsp Italicus bergamot
liqueur or similar

pinch of good-quality
sea salt

ice cubes

prosecco

GLASS

Champagne flute

GARNISH

Orange peel

Mexican in Rome

Behold! A simple twist on the margarita that switches
orange Triple Sec for the aromatic bergamot liqueur Italicus,
unleashing a burst of bubbles.

Pour the tequila, lime juice, and bergamot liqueur into a
Boston shaker. Add the sea salt and fill with ice cubes. Shake
vigorously until cold and fine strain into the glass. Top with
prosecco and garnish with an orange peel. Scrumptious!

2 oz five-year-old rum
1 oz guava juice
1 tbsp lime juice
2 tsp ginger cordial
crushed ice
cava

Highball or collins

Slice of ginger,
lime wheel

Guava Glow

Simple yet highly effective, thanks to big, bold flavors—almost like a rum mule but with an earthy cookie-twist coming from the cava. Tropical and tantalizing!

Pour the rum, guava and lime juices, and ginger cordial into the glass and fill with crushed ice. Top up with a little cava and gently mix. Add more crushed ice and garnish with a slice of ginger and a lime wheel. Feel the glow.

INGREDIENTS

1 oz tequila blanco

1 tbsp freshly squeezed
lime juice

4 tsp freshly squeezed
grapefruit juice

2 tsp agave syrup

ice cubes

sparkling cider

GLASS

Champagne flute

GARNISH

Freshly squeezed
lime juice, sea salt flakes,
chunky slice
of grapefruit

Whizz Paloma Fizz

The Paloma is a classic tequila cocktail pepped
up with lime and grapefruit soda. This recipe is whizzed
up with sparkling cider, which enhances and enriches
the flavor. It works like a base booster to balance
with high citrus zing.

Edge the glass with sea salt flakes by wetting the rim of
the glass with a little lime juice and then rolling in the salt.
Make sure to only get the salt on the outside of the glass.
Pour the tequila, lime and grapefruit juices, and agave syrup
into a Boston shaker. Fill with ice and shake until cold.
Fine strain the mixture into a champagne flute and top
with sparkling cider. Garnish with the grapefruit.

INGREDIENTS
1 oz spiced rum
2 tsp lime juice
5 to 6 mint leaves
crushed ice
Franklin & Sons
Rhubarb Tonic Water
with Hibiscus (or any
good tonic water with a
splash of good-quality
rhubarb cordial)

GLASS
Highball or collins

GARNISH
Sprig of mint

Spiced Rhubarb Tonic

Rum and tonic may sound like liquid lunacy.
But the vibrancy of vanilla, cinnamon, and ginger
layered through spiced rum is a thing of baffling
beauty when laced with a light rhubarb tonic.

Pour the rum and lime juice into the glass. Add the
mint leaves and crushed ice and top with the rhubarb
tonic. Churn and stir to mix and crown with more
crushed ice. Garnish with a sprig of freshly picked
mint. Liquid lunacy is officially glorious.

INGREDIENTS
1 oz vodka
1 tsp lychee liqueur
2 tsp lemon juice
4 tsp watermelon juice
ice cubes
soda water

GLASS
Coupette or champagne
saucer

GARNISH
Lemon peel

Soda over Watermelon

Fresh and floral, this exotic lychee and
watermelon blend is strengthened with vodka
and lengthened with a splash of soda.

Pour the vodka, lychee liqueur, and lemon and
watermelon juices into a Boston shaker and fill with
ice. Shake until cold and fine strain into the glass.
Top with soda water and garnish with a lemon peel.
Simplicity and splendor in equal measure.

INGREDIENTS

ice cubes

1 oz Bloody Bens Bloody
Mary mix
or similar

5 oz tomato juice

4 oz (about ½ small can)
non-alcoholic lager

GLASS

Half-pint

GARNISH

Lime wedges and
chile salt (optional;
you can easily make
your own by stirring
chile powder
into salt)

Mini Michelada

(Booze Free)

Mexico's Michelada has always been a seemingly innocent
way to sip beer for breakfast laced through spicy tomato juice.
These days, with so many fantastic non-alcoholic beers out there
such as Big Drop Brewing Co., this mini Michelada is as innocent
as it needs to be. (Of course, if you switch out the zero percent
beer for a naughty lager, I won't judge.) But the very best thing
about this recipe is that the Bloody Bens Bloody Mary mix does
all the hard work for you—and it really is so ludicrously tasty
there's always a bottle in my fridge. Of course, if you can't find a
good prepared mix, Worcestershire sauce will do nicely.

Wipe the edge of the glass with fresh lime wedges and
dip in chile salt. Fill the glass with ice, pour in the Bloody
Mary mix, tomato juice, and lager and stir gently. Indulge!

INGREDIENTS

4 tsp London dry gin

2 tsp cherry brandy

1 oz lime juice

1 tsp Benedictine

4 tsp Pineapple and
Cardamom Reduction
(see page 12)

ice cubes

champagne

GLASS

Sling

GARNISH

Slice of pineapple,
a fresh cherry

Singapore Sparkle

The Singapore Sling—so famous it asks for its
own autograph at parties. First created at the
world-famous Raffles hotel, this version of the
recipe is amped up with champagne and a fiery
kick of cardamom-infused pineapple syrup.

Pour the gin, cherry brandy, lime juice, Benedictine,
and Pineapple and Cardamom Reduction into a Boston
shaker and fill with ice cubes. Shake until cold and fine
strain into the glass. Fill the glass with ice cubes and
top with champagne. Give it a gentle stir to mix and
garnish with a slice of pineapple and a fresh cherry.
Singapore has never felt more portable!

INGREDIENTS
1 oz pastis
2 tsp lemon juice
crémant
4 tsp crème de cassis

GLASS
Champagne flute

GARNISH
Lemon peel

Pastis Goes Pop

Anise and blackcurrant pair as beautifully together as
a hammock and a snooze. Add the gentle refreshment
of citrus and bubbly, and that hazy happiness of
a southern French holiday is just one short sip away.

Pour the pastis and lemon juice into the glass. Top
with the crémant until it's around two fingers' width
from the top. Pour in the crème de cassis, et voilà!
Garnish with a twirl of lemon peel and you have a
two-toned drink that's as hazy as holidays.

INGREDIENTS

2 oz white rum

2 tsp lime juice

1 oz mango juice

1 tsp Simple Sugar
Syrup (see page 11)

ice cubes

cava

GLASS

Highball or collins

GARNISH

Slice of lime,
sprig of mint

Mango Spritz

Tropical mango has the knack of making it feel sunny
even when surrounded by drizzle and puddles. With mellow
Caribbean white rum eliding with the savory
twist of Spanish sparkling cava, the Mango Spritz is
a one-way ticket to relaxation.

Pour the rum, lime and mango juices, and Simple Sugar Syrup
into the glass. Fill with cubed ice and top with cava. Give
it a gentle stir to mix and garnish with a freshly sliced
lime wheel and a sprig of mint. And relax!

We all need fast and fabulous fizz to keep delivering the dancing, and these energizers will have you singing the dawn chorus! Crank up that stereo. . . .

Disco

07

INGREDIENTS

4 tsp egg white

4 tsp lemon juice

2 tsp Orange Reduction
(see page 11)

1 oz sloe gin

ice cubes

1 oz sparkling wine

GLASS

Coupette or champagne
saucer

GARNISH

Orange peel

Sloe and Low Fizz

Sparkling wine has a defining zestiness to it, thanks
to Britain's marginal—some say cool—climate. Combined with
zesty citrus and sweet sloe, this fizz is as classy as a waltz
and as invigorating as ABBA.

Combine the egg white, lemon juice, Orange Reduction, and
sloe gin in a Boston shaker, add a single ice cube, and shake
until the ice cube stops rattling. Separate the tin, refill with
ice, and shake until cold. In the champagne saucer, pour the
sparkling wine, top by fine straining in the shaken mixture,
and garnish with an orange peel. Zap!

INGREDIENTS
2 tsp vodka
2 tsp triple sec
2 tsp white rum
2 tsp gin
2 tsp tequila blanco

1 tbsp lemon juice
1 tbsp Spiced
Mango Reduction
(see page 13)
ice cubes
prosecco

GLASS
Highball or collins

GARNISH
Slice of lemon

Dancing to Long Island

The Long Island Iced Tea, with rum, vodka, gin, and orange liqueur is as punchy as dancercize class. This sparkling iteration keeps the flavors focused on a fruity lightness— with a shimmering sparkle, of course.

Combine the vodka, triple sec, white rum, gin, tequila, lemon juice, and Spiced Mango Reduction in a Boston shaker. Fill with ice cubes and shake until cold. Strain into the glass and top with more ice and the prosecco. Garnish with a slice of lemon.

INGREDIENTS
2 oz Seedlip Grove 42
non-alcoholic spirit or
similar
1 oz chilled fresh orange
juice
sparkling water

GLASS
Champagne flute

GARNISH
Half-slice of orange

MiNOsa

(Booze Free)

Ellie Sparrow and the magical team at Seedlip are busy
creating non-alcoholic cocktails that not only taste amazing
but look striking. And what's even more wonderful is that
being free of booze isn't necessarily the most important
thing about them—in fact, I'd say the most important thing
about the MiNOsa is that it tastes tremendous
and couldn't be simpler to create.

Add the Seedlip Grove, orange juice, and sparkling water
to the glass, stir gently, garnish with the orange, and serve.
Simple and highly effective to jig around with.

INGREDIENTS

1 oz Midori
melon liqueur
or similar

4 tsp lemon juice

1 tbsp Oleo Saccharum
(see page 15)

ice cubes

prosecco, chilled

GLASS

Champagne flute

GARNISH

Lemon peel

Light Show

Packed with mellow, fruity fizz, this refresher is
as invigorating as taking a shower in disco lights!

Combine the Midori, lemon juice, and Oleo Saccharum
in a Boston shaker. Fill with ice and shake until cold.
Fine strain into the champagne flute and top with
chilled prosecco. Garnish with a slice of lemon peel.

INGREDIENTS

4 tsp gin

1 tbsp lemon juice

2 tsp blue curaçao

cava

2 tsp grenadine syrup

The Discotizer

The Discotizer is my nickname on the dance floor.
With the right tune and the right glass in my hand,
I become an unstoppable force of whirling arms,
high kicks, and, on occasion, forward rolls. This
drink will transform you into The Discotizer.

Pour the gin, lemon juice, and blue curaçao into the
champagne flute, and give it a gentle stir to mix. Top
with cava, leaving a gap about two fingers wide to the
top of the glass. Add the grenadine, which will sink to
the bottom, unleashing a deep purple tone. Garnish
with an orange peel. The Discotizer is ready.

INGREDIENTS

4 tsp lemon juice

1 tbsp Oleo Saccharum
(see page 15)

ice cubes

soda water

2 tsp grenadine syrup

GLASS

Highball or collins

GARNISH

Twist of lemon
peel, maraschino
or fresh cherries

Bassey Temple

(Booze Free)

Dame Shirley Bassey has her own pink sparkling
cocktail created by The Mandarin Bar in London.
The Shirley Temple is booze free and takes its cue
from grenadine. This mocktail is a twist on both—
and it's nothing short of symphonic.

In a glass, pour the lemon juice and Oleo
Saccharum. Fill with ice and top with soda.
Finish by pouring in the grenadine and garnish
with a twist of lemon peel and cherries.

INGREDIENTS
1 tbsp white rum
1 tbsp blue curaçao
1 tbsp lemon juice
2 tsp Pineapple and
Cardamom Reduction
(see page 12)
ice cubes
cava

GLASS
Highball or collins

GARNISH
Pineapple leaves

Blue Bubble Punch

Blue and brilliant, this punch is primed with bold
flavors and a cascade of fizz. Go steady on this one—
it didn't get its nickname, Disco Fuel, for nothing. . . .

Add the rum, blue curaçao, lemon juice, and Pineapple
and Cardamom Reduction to a Boston shaker. Fill with
ice and shake until cold. Strain into the highball glass and fill
with ice. Top with cava and garnish with pineapple leaves.

1 tbsp vodka

1 tbsp crème de pêche

2 dashes of
orange bitters

2 tsp lime juice

2 tsp Cranberry
Reduction (see page
13) or store-bought
cranberry syrup

ice cubes

soda water

GLASS

Champagne flute

GARNISH

Lime peel

Laser Beams

Great cocktails, like great dancers, rely on a perfect
sense of balance. The lime juice in this cocktail
transforms it from a respectable living room disco
into a full-on laser beams all-night extravaganza.

In a Boston shaker, combine the vodka, crème de
pêche, orange bitters, lime juice, and Cranberry Reduction.
Fill with ice and shake until cold. Fine strain into the
glass and top with soda water. Garnish with a lime peel.
Unleash your inner spandex.

INGREDIENTS

1 oz plus ½ tsp gin

2 tsp lemon juice

1 oz prosecco, plus more
to top up

2 tsp tomato juice

1 tbsp orange juice

1 oz Bloody Bens
Bloody Mary mix
or similar

ice cubes

GLASS

Martini

GARNISH

Dehydrated
orange wheel

Discos at Dawn

When you're still dancing as dawn rises, at some point it's
time to change gears and shift into the realm of the Bloody
Mary. Bloody Bens Bloody Mary mix is my absolute favorite
for spicing up anything to do with tomatoes and this rather
precise recipe came to me via dear Ben himself. In fact,
we may or may not have been dancing together
at dawn at the time this cocktail was invented. . . .

Shake all the ingredients vigorously (preferably while still
dancing) in your Boston shaker with ice. Strain gently into the
glass and top up with prosecco. Garnish with a dehydrated
orange wheel. Keep dancing. Ask for another one.

TO MAKE A NON-ALCOHOLIC VERSION

Switch the gin for Seedlip Spice 94 and the prosecco for
Fever-Tree Mediterranean tonic water—it's a ruddy marvelous
booze-free drink that seems to help enormously with sitting
down after an extended boogaloo.

INGREDIENTS

1 tbsp lemon vodka
(Ketel One Citroen is
good, but your favorite
lemon vodka will work
just fine)

1 tbsp triple sec

2 tsp lime juice

2 tsp Cranberry
and Vanilla Reduction
(see page 13)

ice cubes

champagne

GLASS

Coupette or champagne
saucer

GARNISH

Orange peel

San Fran Sparkler

The San Francisco cocktail is a vibrant classic
with banana and orange uniting in a bid to
outdance each other in a flavorsome face-off.
But this recipe is far more zesty and adds
the buzz of bubbles to kick up your heels.

Combine the vodka, triple sec, lime juice, and
Cranberry and Vanilla Reduction in a Boston shaker.
Fill with ice and shake until cold. Fine strain into the
champagne saucer and top with champagne.
Garnish with orange peel and strut your stuff!

Packed with acrobatic aromatics,
vibrant veg, and floral fun, these sparkling
sunny stunners are designed to
create a sense of unwinding relaxation
with the garden in full bloom.

The
Garden

08

INGREDIENTS

2 tsp lime juice,
plus an extra squeeze

2 oz tequila blanco

1 oz carrot juice

1 oz freshly squeezed
grapefruit juice

ice cubes

cava

GLASS

Highball or collins

GARNISH

Sea salt flakes,
chile flakes, slice
of grapefruit (optional)

Jimador Spritz

Jimadors are the dedicated farmers in Mexico who
harvest the agave plants for tequila and mezcal—
and for this recipe I warmly recommend tracking down
100 percent blue agave tequila to achieve the perfect flavor.
After all, this drink is a celebration of the
jimadors' hard work in the great outdoors. *¡Salud!*

Mix the sea salt and chile flakes together. Wet the edge
of the glass with a little lime juice and roll in the chile-
salt flakes. Pour in the tequila, lime juice, carrot juice, and
grapefruit juice. Fill with ice. Top with cava and give it
a gentle stir to mix. Finish with a slice of grapefruit.

INGREDIENTS
1 oz freshly squeezed Granny Smith apple juice
1 oz freshly squeezed rhubarb juice
1 tbsp honey
ice cubes

non-alcoholic sparkling wine (sparkling lemonade will do as an alternative)

GLASS
Champagne flute

GARNISH
Rhubarb ribbon

Bees Crumble

(Booze Free)

The extra effort of freshly squeezed apple and rhubarb is well worth it here for a real sense of vibrancy that balances beautifully with honey's natural unctuousness. And as a beekeeper, I'm all about the honey!

Combine the apple and rhubarb juices with the honey in a Boston shaker. Fill with ice and shake until the tin is cold. Fine strain into the flute and top with the non-alcoholic sparkling wine or lemonade. Garnish with a ribbon of rhubarb.

ice cubes

2 oz Seedlip Garden 108 or similar non-alcoholic spirit

4 tsp elderflower cordial

squeeze of lime juice

Fever-Tree Refreshingly Light Indian tonic water (or other tonic water of choice)

Wine

Slices of cucumber

Garden Spritz

(Booze Free)

Seedlip cleverly sucks the very spirit of the garden into its non-alcoholic creations, and this cocktail revels in the fresh, light fragrance of summer.

Add a few cubes of ice to the glass, followed by the Seedlip Garden, elderflower cordial, and squeeze of fresh lime juice and then top with tonic water. Stir and add a couple of cucumber slices to garnish.

INGREDIENTS

2 oz spiced rum

4 tsp fresh
rhubarb juice

2 tsp lemon juice

4 tsp vanilla syrup

ice cubes

soda water

GLASS

Highball or collins

GARNISH

Rhubarb ribbon

Rum and Rhubarb Collins

A Collins tends to be sour in some way and rhubarb is
a particular favorite for creating an acceptable edge to the
drink. And seeing as it grows rampantly in my garden,
I discovered a way to mimic the flavors of rhubarb and
custard in a way that isn't as silly as it sounds!

In the glass, combine the rum, rhubarb and lemon juices,
and vanilla syrup. Fill with ice and top with soda. Give it a
gentle stir to mix and garnish with a ribbon of rhubarb.

INGREDIENTS
4 tsp vodka
2 tsp crème
de violette
2 tsp lemon juice
dash of orange bitters
ice cubes
champagne

GLASS
Champagne flute

GARNISH
Edible flowers

Sky Diving

I love gazing at the sky, whether it's noon or midnight. Endlessly alluring, delicately fascinating, whether the swallows are darting overhead or stars are blinking benevolently from the deep, I wanted to try and create a sparkling drink to reflect a similar level of intrigue, taking inspiration from the classic sky-blue Aviation cocktail. Dive into the sky!

Combine the vodka, crème de violette, lemon juice, and orange bitters in a Boston shaker. Fill with ice and shake until cold, then fine strain into the glass and top with champagne. Garnish with edible flowers—pansies in particular.

INGREDIENTS

4 tsp gin

4 tsp cherry
brandy liqueur

1 tbsp lemon juice

1 oz freshly squeezed
beet juice

ice cubes

medium-dry
apple cider

GLASS

Highball or collins

GARNISH

Slice of apple

Fruity Rooty

This recipe is easy to execute and salutes the earthy
oddness of the beet, which balances between
fruity and savory as no other root vegetable can.
It's wild—and wonderful.

In the glass, combine the gin, cherry brandy, lemon juice,
and beet juice. Fill with ice cubes and top with the cider.
Give it a gentle stir to mix and garnish with a slice of apple.

4 tsp egg white

1 oz lemon juice

4 tsp elderflower liqueur

2 tsp Simple Sugar
Syrup (see page 11)

1 oz freshly squeezed
cucumber juice

1 oz gin

ice cubes

2 oz prosecco

GLASS

Wine

GARNISH

Cucumber ribbon

Garden Glory

The botanicals of gin, floral elderflower, and peachy prosecco all surround this sparkler with a sense of fragrance and finesse. If you have a hammock nearby, now is the time to deploy it— and refresh yourself with a glass or two of Garden Glory.

Combine the egg white, lemon juice, elderflower liqueur, Simple Sugar Syrup, cucumber juice, and gin in a Boston shaker. Add a single ice cube and shake until the ice cube stops rattling. Separate the tin, refill with ice and shake again until cold. Pour the prosecco into the glass and fine strain the shaken mixture over the top. Garnish with a ribbon of cucumber.

2 oz Uncle Duke's single grain whisky (or other decent whisky)

1 oz freshly squeezed Granny Smith apple juice

1 tsp lemon juice

ice cubes

ginger beer

Highball or collins

Slice of apple

Scotch Granny

My Scottish granny Mary-Pat was an immense fan of both gardening and all drinks. She lived to be just a few years shy of a hundred and particularly loved whisky at the end of a long day's weeding. I can't say for sure if she ever sipped on the candied-orange notes of Uncle Duke's, but it seems a half-decent excuse to raise this glass to the glory of grannies and their glorious gardens.

In the glass, combine the whisky and apple and lemon juices. Fill with ice and top with the ginger beer. Give the drink a gentle stir to mix and garnish with a slice of apple.

1 oz Dubonnet
sweet vermouth
or similar

1 tsp lemon juice

4 strawberries, hulled

3 basil leaves

ice cubes

prosecco

Champagne flute

Slice of strawberry,
basil leaves

Strawberry and Basil Alfonso

The Alfonso usually has Dubonnet at its heart, and
I adore the aromatic basil boost and fruity strawberry
oomph of this bubbly belter. Bang on for sipping
through the summertime.

In a Boston shaker, combine the vermouth, lemon juice,
strawberries, and basil. Press with a muddler, fill with ice
cubes, and shake until cold. Fine strain into the champagne
flute and top with prosecco. Add a slice of strawberry
and basil leaves to garnish.

INGREDIENTS	GLASS	GARNISH
1 tbsp just-boiled water	Silver julep cup or highball	Sprig of mint
8 mint leaves		
4½ tsp honey		
crushed ice		
ice-cold ginger beer		

Honey and Ginger Julep

(Booze Free)

I love keeping bees, and when they're buzzing about when the mint is rampaging across the garden in the height of summer, you can feel the whole garden is alive with tasty treats. This is the perfect quencher for those warm, wonderful days, with a big hit of ginger to enliven your day.

Mix the freshly boiled water with 2 of the fresh mint leaves and stir to wilt. Stir in the honey and then remove the mint leaves. Leave to cool completely.

Place the remaining 6 fresh mint leaves at the base of a glass. Pack the glass with crushed ice. Pour in the honey syrup, mix, and stir fast. Top up with ice-cold ginger beer. Add more ice to top, and stir again before adding a final sprig of mint.

+ TIPPLE TIP Adding a trickle of bourbon turns this into a naughtier version, if you fancy!

From Christmas Eve to
weddings, holidays, anniversaries,
and birthdays, these recipes
are a riot of color, easy detail,
and invigoration.

Festivals and Celebrations

09

INGREDIENTS

2 oz Aperol
or similar

1 oz fresh
orange juice

1 oz fresh
rhubarb juice

2 oz prosecco

2 tsp Simple Sugar
Syrup (see page 11)

ice cubes

GLASS

Large wine

GARNISH

Slice of orange

Weekend Spritz

Rhubarb and bitter orange ramp up this refresher
for the perfect weekend wonder drink.

Combine the Aperol, orange juice, rhubarb juice, prosecco,
Simple Sugar Syrup, and ice in the glass. Give it a gentle
stir. Add more ice if needed and garnish with a slice
of orange. The weekend has officially begun!

INGREDIENTS

1 oz George's Old
59 gin or similar

1 tsp Pimento
Dram liqueur

2 tsp lemon juice

1 tbsp pomegranate
syrup (or grenadine)

ice cubes

prosecco, chilled

GLASS

Champagne flute

GARNISH

Orange peel studded
with 3 cloves

Christmas Spice

Here's to all the flavors of Christmas in one fruity
and spicy concoction. I recommend George's Old 59
for its cardamom and orange notes, but your pick of
gin will also work just fine.

Pour the gin, Pimento Dram, lemon juice, and pomegranate
syrup into a Boston shaker. Fill with ice and shake until cold.
Fine strain into the champagne flute and top with chilled
prosecco. Garnish with an orange peel studded with cloves.

1 lb 2 oz watermelon,
peel and seeds removed

Highball or collins

Sprig of mint, slice
of watermelon

squeeze of
lemon juice

squeeze of lime juice

crushed ice

2½ oz sparkling
raspberry lemonade

Watermelon and Raspberry Cooler

(Booze Free)

With the feeling of a hot holiday in every eye-catching
cool sip, this is simply superb—whatever the weather.

Mash the watermelon flesh in a bowl. Add the lemon and
lime juices and stir. Press the watermelon through a sieve
into a pitcher, pressing down gently on the pulp to
extract all the juices.

Fill the glass with crushed ice. Pour the watermelon juice into
the glass and top up with raspberry lemonade. Garnish with
a sprig of mint and a slice of watermelon.

INGREDIENTS	GLASS	GARNISH
1 oz Brentingby gin or similar	Champagne flute	Orange peel
2 tsp Monin hibiscus syrup or similar		
2 tsp freshly squeezed orange juice		
2 tsp lemon juice		
ice cubes		
champagne		

Cheers to You

Romance is in the air! Whether it's an anniversary, proposal, or spontaneous celebration of love's limitless wonder, this drink is for you and the one you love. Brentingby gin from Melton Mowbray is the one to pick here for its soft, smooth texture, which some say is thanks to birch being one of its botanicals. All I know for sure is that it feels as slinky as a slow dance.

In a Boston shaker, combine the gin, hibiscus syrup, and orange and lemon juices. Open the tin, fill with ice, and shake until cold. Fine strain into the glass and top with champagne. Garnish with orange peel.

INGREDIENTS

1 oz Bison Grass vodka or similar

4 tsp freshly pressed Granny Smith apple juice

2 tsp elderflower cordial

Simple Sugar Syrup (see page 11), to taste

ice cubes

champagne

GLASS

Coupette or champagne saucer

GARNISH

Apple fan

Say Yes

For the big day, whatever shape or form that may take, celebrate with this fruity and floral spritz. It's as awesome as you are!

Combine the vodka, apple juice, elderflower cordial, and Simple Sugar Syrup in a Boston shaker. Fill with ice and shake until cold. Fine strain into the glass and top with champagne. Garnish with an apple fan. Here's to you!

4 tsp Spiced
Mango Reduction
(see page 13)

2 tsp lime juice

non-alcoholic wine
(a good sparkling
lemonade works as an
alternative), chilled

Champagne flute

Strip of orange peel

The New Addition

(Booze Free)

Is it a boy, a girl, a puppy, or a cat? Who cares with
this booze-free brilliance in your glass!

Pour the Spiced Mango Reduction and lime juice into
the champagne flute and top with chilled non-alcoholic
wine or lemonade. Garnish with a strip of orange peel.
Raise your glass to the new addition.

INGREDIENTS

1 oz pink port

2 tsp Oleo Saccharum
(see page 15)

1 tsp lemon juice

4 tsp cranberry juice

ice cubes

cava

GLASS

Coupette or champagne
saucer

GARNISH

Slice of lemon peel

Crossing the Border

The perfect glass to celebrate moving! Its relatively
low booze content means one or two won't stop you
from unpacking the odd box or slumping into an
armchair, depending on your mood.

Combine the port, Oleo Saccharum, and lemon and
cranberry juices in a Boston shaker. Fill with ice cubes
and shake until cold. Fine strain into the glass and
top with cava. Garnish with a slice of lemon peel.

INGREDIENTS
1 oz advocaat
2 tsp lemon juice
4 tsp vanilla syrup
ice cubes
crémant

GLASS
Coupette or champagne
saucer

GARNISH
Sprig of mint

Spruced-Up Snowball

Christmas without a snowball is like July without a picnic.
Spruced up with crémant and vanilla for a deep sweet tickle,
this is a snowball to melt the hardest heart.

In a Boston shaker, combine the advocaat, lemon juice,
and vanilla syrup. Fill with ice and shake until cold.
Fine strain into the glass and top with crémant,
then garnish with a sprig of mint.

INGREDIENTS

1 oz white rum

4 tsp pink
grapefruit liqueur

4 tsp lime juice

2 tsp Orange Reduction
(see page 11)

dash of Angostura bitters

ice cubes

champagne

GLASS

Tumbler

GARNISH

Slice of orange,
sprig of mint
(optional)

Champagne Birthday Punch

Happy Birthday! Celebrate with the world's most uplifting recipe for punch topped with fizz. You deserve it.

In the glass, build the rum, pink grapefruit liqueur, lime juice, Orange Reduction, and bitters. Fill with ice and top with champagne. Garnish with a slice of orange and mint, if desired. Celebration time!

INGREDIENTS
4 tsp rhubarb syrup
sparkling wine, chilled

GLASS
Champagne flute

GARNISH
A fresh raspberry

English Sparkle

This cocktail is all about the freshness and vibrancy of the
English summer. Wine has been made on English shores since
Roman times, nearly two thousand years ago, and our climate
is perfectly suited to create beautiful bubbly that's bright and
charged with electrifying refreshment.

Pour the rhubarb syrup into the flute and top with
the chilled sparkling wine. Garnish the glass
with one fresh raspberry and serve.

Thanks

The bubbles in my life have been popping splendidly thanks
to the kind help, support, and professional wisdom of Lizzy Gray,
Louise McKeever, Gordon Wise, Niall Harman, Sophie Smith,
Ellie James, Tim Garrett, Rob Allison, Ellie Sparrow, Ben Walton,
Kim Lightbody, Lucy Sykes-Thompson, Tamara Vos, Jo Harris,
Lucy Harrison, Kate Wanwimolruk, the late Barney, and the early
Busby. Thank you all very much—drinks are on me.

Biography

Olly Smith is a multi-award-winning wine writer and
broadcaster. He is known for his regular appearances on
BBC1's *Saturday Kitchen* and presents his own shows on
BBC Radio 2. Olly writes a weekly wine column for the
Mail on Sunday and hosts his own podcast, *A Glass With . . .*,
which kicked off with pop star P!nk. Olly is listed in Debrett's
500 as one of the 500 most influential people in the UK.

Olly has been crowned the International Wine and Spirits
Communicator of the Year and won Drinks Writer of the Year
at the 2016 and 2017 Great British Food Awards. He is the Drinks
Ambassador for the Ideal Home Show and appears at his own
series of Three Wine Men events. He has designed his own
range of glassware, including a glass especially for fizz!
(Available online at ollysmith.com)

With his own award-winning chain of Glass House wine bars
aboard P&O Cruises, and as the author of four books and the
creator of a successful wine app, the only thing Olly is more
enthusiastic about than fizz is sharing it.

ollysmith.com